CW01335376

Good Choices, Bad Choices

Jean Stapleton

10 9 8 7 6 5 4 3 2 1

Copyright © 2020 Jean Stapleton
Paperback ISBN: 978-1-5271-0527-0

Published by Christian Focus Publications,
Geanies House, Fearn, Tain, Ross-shire,
IV20 1TW, Scotland, U.K.
www.christianfocus.com;
email: info@christianfocus.com

Cover design by Daniel van Straaten
Cover illustration and page layout by Daniel van Straaten
Printed in Turkey by Imago

All rights reserved. No part of this publication may be reproduced, stored in a retrieval system, or transmitted, in any form, by any means, electronic, mechanical, photocopying, recording or otherwise without the prior permission of the publisher or a licence permitting restricted copying. In the U.K. such licences are issued by the Copyright Licensing Agency, 4 Battlebridge Lane, London, SE1 2HX. www.cla.co.uk

Scripture taken from the New King James Version. Copyright © 1982 by Thomas Nelson, Inc. Used by permission. All rights reserved.

CONTENTS

Introduction	5
The First Wrong Choice	7
Two Brothers, Different Choices	11
Noah: A Saving Choice	14
Babel: The Choice to Rebel	17
Abraham Chose to Obey God	19
Lot: A Choice that Brought Trouble	22
Rebekah Chooses to go on a Journey	25
Esau's Careless Choice	28
Jacob Chose to Deceive	30
Joseph's Brothers Chose Hatred	33
Joseph's Choice to do Right	35
Pharaoh Chooses his Prime Minister	38
Joseph's Choice to Forgive	41
The Midwives' Brave Choice	44
Moses Chose Suffering	46
Pharaoh: A Proud Choice	49
The People's Choice: Disobedience	52
Korah Chose to Rebel	55
Rahab: A Choice of Faith	58
Achan: A Choice of Covetousness	61
The Gibeonites Chose to Deceive	64
Another Choice for the People	66
Gideon and the Men who Chose to go Home	69

Samson's Choice of Unhelpful People 72
A Husband's Choice and a Widow's Choice 75
Orpah and Ruth..78
2 Relations 2 Choices 80
Hannah Chose to Pray 83
Samuel Chose to be Faithful to God........................... 86
David Chose to Trust God.. 89
David Chose not to Take Revenge 92
Jonathan Chose to be a True Friend........................... 95
David's Seriously Wrong Choice 98
Absalom: A Rebellious Choice....................................101
King Solomon: Two Choices 104
The Queen who Chose to See for Herself.................107
Rehoboam Chose to Follow Bad Advice 110
The King who Chose to Set up Idols 112
Naaman Almost Made a Wrong Choice 115
Gehazi Chose Greed and Deceit 117

INTRODUCTION

The Bible tells us about many people who made choices. Some were good, wise choices. Some were wrong, foolish choices. When we have choices to make, it is important that we ask God to help us to make wise choices. As we become adults, where we live, what work we do, who we marry, are all important choices. If we are Christians, we will pray that God will guide us in our decision-making.

The Bible teaches us that God always does what He says He will do. It is a great comfort to know that God's plans and purposes are not changed by men and women who make wrong or foolish choices. In a way that we cannot understand, God rules over everything so that His promises are always fulfilled.

Jean Stapleton

Dedication:
To Beryl who thought about choices

THE FIRST WRONG CHOICE

Adam and Eve, the first man and woman created by God, lived in a perfect world. They could tend the beautiful garden that was their home, without discomfort or tiredness. They could enjoy each other's company with no unkind thoughts or words. They knew nothing of illness or fear of death.

Into this perfect situation came an intruder – a serpent, used by the devil to tempt Adam and Eve to disobey God. God had given Adam just one command, one rule that he must keep. He must not eat fruit from one particular tree which was called "the tree of the knowledge of good and evil". Keeping this one rule would show his willingness to obey the God who had given him life and every good thing to enjoy. Breaking God's command would bring death.

The serpent tempted Eve by presenting the idea that God was withholding something good from her. The fruit that God had forbidden, would actually make her wise, like God Himself.

Eve had a choice to make. Should she trust the God who had made her and given her everything she needed? Surely the God who had created the world was wise and would know what was best for her. Or should she believe the serpent, who dared to contradict what God had said?

Eve looked at the tree of the knowledge of good and evil. The fruit was attractive, it looked good. She reached out and took some fruit, she ate it and gave some to Adam and he ate it. In that simple act, Adam and Eve rebelled against their loving Creator. Instead of obeying God, they had obeyed the devil who hates God and hates everything that is good. The devil had deceived Eve. He had lied to her, and much sorrow was to follow her choice.

Adam and Eve felt ashamed and sewed leaves together to cover themselves. Worse still, when they heard God's voice, they hid among the trees, as if they could hide from God. Instead of confessing that they had done wrong, Adam blamed Eve for giving him the fruit, and Eve blamed the serpent.

The choice Adam and Eve made on that day, changed everything. Sin, sickness, sorrow and death came into the world. Everyone born into the world since, except the Lord Jesus, is sinful and does, says and thinks things that are wrong.

READ: GENESIS 2-3; MATTHEW 1:21; REVELATION 12:9
QUESTIONS:
1. How do we know that the serpent was really the devil speaking to Eve? (Read Revelation 12:9)
2. Genesis 3:15 is picture language about someone who will overcome the devil. This is the first promise in the Bible of a Saviour. Who is the promised Saviour? (Matthew 1:21)
3. What is the difference between Adam's work in Genesis 2:15, and in 3:17-18?

EXTRA

ADAM AND EVE'S CHOICE AND GOD'S PLAN FOR PEOPLE TO BE "LIKE HIM" (GENESIS 1:26)

God is perfectly pure and holy. The human race had become sinful. Had the devil spoiled God's plan?

In Revelation 13:8, the Lord Jesus is called "The Lamb slain from the foundation of the world". This teaches us that from the beginning, God knew what He would do.

The Lord Jesus, God's own Son, would take sin's punishment for everyone who trusts in Him. He did this when He died on the cross so that we can be forgiven.

God sends His Holy Spirit to those who trust in the Lord Jesus. The Holy Spirit works in their lives, making them more like the Lord Jesus. The Bible calls this "sanctification". It begins when someone becomes a Christian and continues until the end of their life in this world. In this way God carries on His plan of making people "like Him".

TWO BROTHERS, DIFFERENT CHOICES

Cain and Abel were brothers, the sons of Adam and Eve. Abel became a shepherd whilst Cain was a grower of crops. They both knew that they should bring an offering to God. Sin had come into the world when Adam and Eve disobeyed God. Sin stops us knowing God as our Friend. He can only be approached in the way that He lays down.

Abel brought a sheep as his offering, so that his sin could be forgiven. The sheep had to be killed, because the punishment for sin is death (Romans 6:23). When Adam and Eve sinned, God had promised that He would send a Saviour (Genesis 3:15). Until that time, He accepted the death of an animal in place of the sinner. God accepted Abel and his offering, because Abel showed that he was trusting in the promised Saviour. He would have understood that the offering he brought, in some way looked forward to what that Saviour would do.

Cain was very angry because his brother was accepted by God, but he was not. Cain did a terrible thing. He killed his brother Abel. God knew what Cain had done, although Cain told a lie and said that he did not know where his brother was. Adam and Eve were the first man and woman that God created. They made the terrible choice to disobey God. After this, everyone born into the world, except the Lord Jesus, is a sinner. Adam and Eve could see the results of their own sinful action in the life of their son Cain: murder and lies. How sorrowful they must have been to lose one son because of the sinful actions of another son.

In the Book of Hebrews there is a list of people who, in Old Testament days, had faith in God. Abel's name is the first on that list. The sacrifice that he offered showed his faith in God's way of forgiveness. We no longer have to bring an offering to God. The Lord Jesus died in place of all those who have faith (put their trust) in Him. Through faith in the Lord Jesus, all our sin can be forgiven.

READ: GENESIS 4:1-16; HEBREWS 11:4
QUESTIONS:
1. Why was Cain angry with his brother? (Genesis 4:3-5)
2. What sins did Cain commit? (Genesis 4:8-9)
3. Why did Abel bring the right offering? (Hebrews 11:4)

NOAH: A SAVING CHOICE

Noah did not live in good days. There was violence everywhere and the people around him continually allowed evil things to fill their thoughts. How had the world at that time got into such a bad state? The people had turned away from God. Left to themselves, they followed their own sinful ways, hating and hurting one another.

Noah was different from the people around him. He did not follow their evil ways. And yet, even Noah was not without sin. We read that he "found grace" from God. Grace means kindness that we do not deserve.

God told Noah that because the people had become so evil, they would be destroyed by a great flood. God gave Noah instructions for building an ark: a huge wooden boat, about 140 metres long and about 23 metres wide.

Noah, his wife and his three sons and their wives were to go into the ark with a male and female of every sort of animal, except for certain ones which were to be saved in sevens.

Noah obeyed God. It took him a long time to build the ark. A flood had never been seen on the earth before. How the people must have mocked him as he toiled day after day. However much he warned them, no one took any notice. Only Noah and his wife, his three sons and their wives were saved.

Noah chose to believe and obey God, and so he and his family were saved from the great flood which covered the whole earth. The Lord Jesus spoke about the time that Noah lived, before the flood. He said that life would be just like that, before His return to earth. People would be living with no thought of God, right up to the day of His coming. It will then be too late for anyone to be saved from the punishment for their sin. Now is the time to trust in the Lord Jesus, and to look forward without fear of His return.

READ: GENESIS 6:5-14; 7:5-16; MATTHEW 24:37-39; HEBREWS 11:7
QUESTIONS:
1. Find two reasons why God sent the great flood. (Genesis 6:5, 13)

2. Who decided that the opportunity to enter the ark would end, and that the door would be closed? (Genesis 7:16)
3. What two things did Noah have that the people all around him did not have? (Hebrews 11:7)

BABEL: THE CHOICE TO REBEL

When God created the first man, Adam, He told him that his descendants should fill the earth. Then after the flood, God repeated this instruction to Noah and his sons. However, as more people were born and the population began to grow again, the people decided they would have more power if they remained together. Their idea was to build a city with a great tower. This they believed would make them secure. They had a powerful leader – a man named Nimrod (Genesis 10:8-10).

So the people deliberately chose to rebel against God. God's purpose for men and women was that they should take charge of the world He had made. They were intended to live in all parts of the world and care for all the living creatures. Babel is the true story of men and women rebelling against their Creator. God has perfect knowledge. He knows all that has ever happened, or will happen. God always carries out His purposes, in spite of the wrong choices people make. So God caused the people to begin speaking in different languages. This caused such confusion that the building of the city was abandoned. People began to move to different lands. Groups of people speaking the same language stayed together. From these groups came all the nations of the world.

In the time of Noah and at the time of Babel, we see that mankind does not want to obey God. The first sin, in Eden, was disobedience.

We all have sinful hearts and want to go our own way (Isaiah 53: 6). The Bible tells us that God is good. He knows what is best for the people He has made. To rebel against God, wanting our own way instead of His, is both wrong and foolish.

READ: GENESIS 1:26-28; 9:1; 11:1-9
QUESTIONS:
1. Why was the city and the great tower being built? (Genesis 11:4)
2. What had God planned that men and women were to do? (Genesis 1:26-28)
3. What did God do that brought the building to an end and caused His plan to be carried out? (Genesis 11:7-9)

ABRAHAM CHOSE TO OBEY GOD

Abraham lived in the city of Ur, in the country we know as Iraq. God told him that he must leave his home and move to a land that God would show him.

Not knowing exactly where his future home would be, Abraham set out. His father, his wife and his nephew travelled north with him to the city of Haran (Haran was situated in what is now Northern Iraq).

Abraham's father died in Haran, and Abraham then travelled south into the land of Canaan, with his wife and his nephew.

God told Abraham that He would give this land to his descendants. Abraham had chosen to obey God. God had chosen Abraham to begin a new nation. Into this nation the Son of God would be born.

Many years passed. Abraham and Sarah waited twenty-five years for their son, Isaac, to be born. Then there came a day when Abraham's choice of obedience to God was tested. God instructed Abraham to go to a certain place and offer Isaac as a sacrifice there. The people who lived in Canaan at that time, did sacrifice their children to the idols they worshipped. God had never asked that such a thing should be done for His worship.

Abraham obeyed promptly. On the third day of the journey, he saw the place that God had told him of. Abraham built an altar there and laid his son on the altar. He had waited twenty-five years for his son whom he loved. All God's promises to his descendants depended on Isaac continuing the family. And yet Abraham obeyed God.

An angel spoke to Abraham, telling him not to harm Isaac. Abraham had shown that he loved and obeyed God. Through this, God had given a picture of what He would do, when He sent His beloved Son into the world, to die on the cross.

Abraham's obedience was based on his faith – he believed God. His faith was proved to be genuine by his obedience.

READ: GENESIS 12:1-7; HEBREWS 11:8-19; MATTHEW 1:1, 16; JOHN 3:16
QUESTIONS:
1. Who was born from Abraham's descendants who would be a blessing to people throughout the world? (Genesis 12:3; Matthew 1:1, 16)
2. What did Abraham believe that God would do, if he made an offering of his son Isaac? (Hebrews 11:19)
3. Who did give His Son, so that whoever believes in Him would have everlasting life? (John 3:16 – Make sure that you memorise this verse.)

LOT: A CHOICE THAT BROUGHT TROUBLE

Lot was the nephew who travelled with Abraham from Ur to Haran and then to Canaan. Eventually, Lot made his home in the land of Canaan near to Abraham and Sarah.

Abraham and Lot both owned a lot of animals and they had men who looked after the animals for them. So many herds and flocks of animals needed a lot of food and water and the men looking after them began to quarrel about this.

Abraham did not want this to cause trouble between him and his nephew, so he suggested that they move apart from each other. Abraham kindly gave Lot the choice of which part of the land he would like to settle in. Lot looked east towards the River Jordan. He saw that it would be a good place for his animals, well-watered by the river. So Lot moved eastward and then moved south near to the city of Sodom.

It seemed that Lot had made a good choice of rich pasture land and a good water supply. But the city of Sodom was a very sinful place, and

Lot became involved in great trouble. There was fighting between two groups of local kings and Lot was taken captive. When Abraham heard the news, he took 318 men with him to rescue Lot. Abraham actually rescued all the captives and property that had been taken.

Worse was to follow. The evil of two cities, Sodom and Gomorrah, was so great that God decided that they must be destroyed.

Abraham prayed that God would not destroy the cities if even 50 good people lived there. He continued praying, that maybe there would only be 45, 40, 30, 20 or even just 10 good people there. God promised that for the sake of only 10 good people, He would not destroy those cities.

It seemed that not even ten good people could be found. But God remembered Abraham's prayer and He sent two angels to bring Lot and his family out of Sodom, where he was then living. Some of Lot's family took no notice when he told them that they must leave the city. Only his wife and two of his daughters were willing to go with him.

Even then Lot would not hurry so the angels brought them out of the city. The angels told them that they must hurry and that they must not look back. Lot's wife disobeyed and looked back towards Sodom, and there she died.

Lot's choice had brought him a lot of trouble and a lot of unhappiness.

READ: GENESIS 18:20-33; 19:12-26.
QUESTIONS:
1. What did Abraham do when he knew that Sodom was to be destroyed? (Genesis 18:23-32)
2. What did Lot's sons-in-law think about his warning? (Genesis 19:14)
3. In what way did God show kindness to Lot and his family? (Genesis 19:16)

REBEKAH CHOOSES TO GO ON A JOURNEY

God gave wonderful promises to Abraham's family. Because of this, Abraham knew that it was important that his son, Isaac, did not marry a woman from Canaan who worshipped idols. He sent his most trusted servant on a long journey to the place where his own relatives lived in Haran. The servant was to bring back a wife for Isaac. Abraham assured him that God would help him.

After travelling on camels for about five hundred miles, the servant and his helpers waited by a well at Haran. As he stood by the well, the servant prayed. In Genesis Chapter 24, you can read how God answered that prayer, so that Abraham's brother's granddaughter, Rebekah, brought him and the men with him, to her home.

When Rebekah's father and her brother heard about the servant's prayer and how God had answered him, they knew that they must let Rebekah go with him.

The next morning Abraham's servant was eager to set out on the journey back. Rebekah's family wanted her to stay with them for a few more days, but they decided to ask her if she was willing to go. Now was the time for Rebekah to decide what she would do. The servant had told the family all about Abraham and Isaac, but Rebekah had never seen them. If she travelled into the land of Canaan, she would be a long way from her home and the place where she had grown up. But she knew that her father and her brother both believed that God had guided Abraham's servant to meet her.

The Bible does not tell us how Rebekah made her choice, but she must have realised that it was a wonderful thing to have been chosen by God to be Isaac's wife. Rebekah's answer to the question "will you go with this man?" was simple, "I will go."

She did marry Isaac and the Bible tells us that Isaac loved her. The choice that Rebekah made had consequences that she could not have imagined. Rebekah and Isaac's son, Jacob, was given a new name by God: Israel. He had twelve sons whose families became the twelve tribes of Israel. Israel became a nation and it was to that nation that God sent His Son, the Lord

Jesus Christ. This was what God had promised Abraham, two thousand years before Jesus was born in Bethlehem.

READ: GENESIS 12:1-3; GENESIS 24; MATTHEW 1:1, 16
QUESTIONS:
1. What did Rebekah do that showed the servant that God had answered his prayer? (Genesis 24:12-21)
2. In what way was Rebekah related to Abraham? (Genesis 24:15)
3. How did Rebekah manage the long journey to Canaan? (Genesis 24:61)
4. Find the words in Genesis 12:3 that tell us that God promised that a descendant of Abraham would be a blessing to people all over the world. Who was this? (Matthew 1:1, 16)

ESAU'S CARELESS CHOICE

Isaac and Rebekah had twin boys named Esau and Jacob. At that time the oldest boy would grow up to be the next head of the family. Esau was the oldest twin, but before the twins were born God explained to Rebekah that things would be different in this family. The youngest twin would be the head of the family after Isaac.

As they grew up, Esau and Jacob were very different. Esau liked to be outside hunting. Jacob took more interest in the life of the family. As we read more about their lives it does seem that Jacob understood more about the importance of God's promises to his grandfather, Abraham, than Esau had.

One day Esau came home from hunting, very hungry. Jacob was cooking lentil stew. Esau asked for some. Before Jacob would give food to his brother, he asked him for his birthright. This was something special. When the father died, the oldest son would have twice as much of the inheritance as any other son. He then became the head of the family.

Esau had a choice to make. Should he give away his special place in the family, for a plate of stew? Esau, hungry and tired, decided that as he was dying for want of food, he would let his brother have his birthright.

So let's think, who cared most about this family and God's promises? Would Esau really have died without his meal? (He was healthy enough to be out hunting all day.) Was it right for Jacob to ask for his brother's birthright?

The Bible tells us that "Esau despised his birthright" (Genesis 25:34). Hebrews 12:16 calls Esau a godless person, who "for one morsel of food sold his birthright".

READ: GENESIS 25:27-34
QUESTIONS:
1. In the reading, what words show how little Esau cared about his birthright?
2. Is there any blame given to Jacob for wanting the birthright?
3. Sometimes people say that Jacob stole Esau's birthright. Does the Bible say this?

JACOB CHOSE TO DECEIVE

Jacob was the son of Isaac and Rebekah and the grandson of Abraham. He had a twin brother, Esau. Rebekah was told by God before the twins were born, that the second one to be born would become the head of the family after his father Isaac (Genesis 25:23). This was unusual, as the first twin being the oldest would normally take his place as the head of the family, when the time came.

As the twins grew up, it was evident that Jacob had more concern for God's promises to Abraham, than Esau did. In fact Esau sold his "birthright" to Jacob in exchange for a meal.

When Isaac was old and almost blind, he decided he should give his blessing to Esau. Isaac felt he should still treat Esau as his eldest son. Rebekah was concerned when she knew what Isaac planned to do. Esau loved hunting, and Rebekah heard Isaac tell him to go after some game and then prepare a tasty meal. Isaac would then give him his blessing.

Rebekah made a plan. She would prepare a meal and Jacob must take it to his father. But

Jacob knew that although his father could not see, he would be able to touch him and realise that it was not Esau who had brought him the meal. So Rebekah brought some of Esau's clothes for Jacob to wear and some goatskin to cover Jacob's hands and his neck.

Esau was more hairy than his brother, so with the skins and the clothes they would be able to trick Isaac into thinking it was Esau who was there and not Jacob. Jacob did all that his mother told him to do. But he was not a child and he could have talked to her about how wrong it was to deceive his father. They were both right to be concerned, but they should have trusted God to carry out His plans, without them involving themselves in lies and deceit.

Jacob did receive Issac's blessing, but Esau was so angry when he knew what had happened, that Jacob had to go away from home. It would be twenty years before Jacob returned to the land of Canaan. At that time God gave Jacob a new name, "Israel". It was from Jacob's family that the nation of Israel came, and it was from that nation that the Lord Jesus came into the world.

READ: GENESIS 27
QUESTIONS:
1. Whose idea was it, to deceive Isaac? (Genesis 27:6-10)
2. Did Jacob actually lie to his father? (Genesis 27:19-20)
3. Why was Isaac uncertain about which of his two sons was with him? (Genesis 27:21-23)

JOSEPH'S BROTHERS CHOSE HATRED

Joseph was the next to youngest of Jacob's twelve sons. Jacob had a special love for Joseph and this was the cause of his brothers' hatred. Joseph also had two dreams which appeared to mean that his brothers would bow down to him. When they heard about the dreams, they hated him even more.

Jacob sent Joseph to see how his brothers were getting on looking after the flocks. As they saw Joseph coming, they planned to kill him and tell their father that a wild animal was responsible. Reuben, the oldest, stopped the terrible act. He suggested throwing Joseph into a pit instead. His own plan was to rescue him later and take him home. In this way he did at least show some concern for Joseph and for his father.

Reuben's plan was partly carried out. Joseph's coat, a present from his father, was taken from him, and he was thrown into a pit. But Reuben was never able to complete his plan, because another brother named Judah had a different idea. Some traders came along and Judah suggested selling Joseph to them instead of killing him. Reuben must have been away doing something else at the time.

When he returned Joseph had gone. He had been sold as a slave. One thing remained to be done. A young goat was killed, and Joseph's coat was dipped in the blood. Jacob recognised the bloodstained coat and believed that his beloved son had been killed by a wild animal.

The Lord Jesus taught that sinful actions begin in the heart (Mark 7:21). We see this clearly in the life of Joseph's brothers, their hatred and envy almost led to murder and did lead to cruelty and lies.

READ: GENESIS 37
QUESTIONS:
1. Find two reasons why Joseph's brothers hated him. (Genesis 37:3-5; 6-8)
2. What did Reuben plan to do? (Genesis 37:22)
3. Why could Reuben not complete his plan? (Genesis 37:28-29)

JOSEPH'S CHOICE TO DO RIGHT

Joseph's life had completely changed. He had suffered the cruelty of his brothers and the terrifying possibility of being left to die in a pit in the wilderness. Then, roughly handled by traders, he was taken to Egypt, a completely strange land to him. After this, he was put on sale as a slave – what a difference from his home and his father's love.

One of Pharaoh's officers, a man named Potiphar, bought Joseph. As a slave, Joseph had no rights, no choice of what he would do. He belonged to his master and must obey him. But God had not forgotten Joseph.

Potiphar soon realised that he could trust him to look after everything in his household. Life seemed better for Joseph. God was with him and helped him in all that he did. Then a difficult situation arose. His master's wife wanted Joseph to act as if he was her husband.

It may be that Potiphar was so taken up with his work for Pharaoh that he did not give much time to his wife. What could Joseph do? He was a slave, not a free man. However difficult it might make his life, Joseph chose to do what he knew to be right. His master trusted him and he would not betray that trust. Most importantly, he would not sin against God.

When Potiphar came home, his wife told him lies about Joseph. Although he was completely innocent, Joseph was put into prison. Even in prison God was with him and the keeper of the prison put him in charge of the other prisoners. Among those prisoners were two of Pharaoh's servants: his butler and his baker.

One morning the butler and the baker were both looking troubled. They told Joseph the dreams that had troubled them. God gave Joseph understanding and he was able to tell them the meaning of their dreams. What Joseph told them was exactly what happened. The butler was restored to his position, but the baker was put to death.

Joseph asked the butler to speak to Pharaoh for him, as he had done nothing wrong and yet was kept in prison. But two years passed and no release came for Joseph.

READ: GENESIS 39–40
QUESTIONS:
1. What did Potiphar think made Joseph so successful? (Genesis 39:2-3)
2. What two reasons did Joseph have for not doing as his master's wife wanted him to do? (Genesis 39:8-9)
3. What did Joseph ask Pharaoh's butler to do? (Genesis 40:14-15). Did the butler do this? (Genesis 40:23)

PHARAOH CHOOSES HIS PRIME MINISTER

Two years after Pharaoh's butler was set free, something happened that made him remember Joseph. Pharaoh was very troubled about two dreams that he had in one night. When he heard about this, the butler told Pharaoh all about Joseph, how he was able to interpret dreams.

Joseph was immediately sent for, tidied up and brought to Pharaoh. He was careful to tell Pharaoh that it was not him, but God who would give the answer. After listening to Pharaoh's account of his dreams, Joseph told him that both dreams had one meaning. The land of Egypt was going to have seven years of good harvests, followed by seven years of famine.

After explaining the meaning of the dreams, Joseph advised Pharaoh to appoint a wise person to take charge of storing food during the seven good years. Pharaoh saw that this advice was good. He also saw that God had made Joseph wise. He chose to make Joseph the most important person in the land except for himself.

When we first read about Joseph and his brothers, Joseph was seventeen years old. Now at thirty years old, he set about taking charge of storing food in the cities throughout Egypt. He rode in a chariot and people bowed to him. In one day, another tremendous change had taken place in Joseph's life.

Seven years of good harvests passed, and Joseph had made sure that large amounts of grain had been stored. The years of famine began, not only in Egypt but in other countries as well. In the land of Canaan, Jacob heard that there was grain in Egypt. He sent Joseph's ten older brothers to buy grain. He kept the youngest of his sons, Benjamin, at home with him. Jacob had never forgotten the day when Joseph did not return home. That was why he would not allow Benjamin to go to Egypt with his brothers.

Travelling to Egypt, the brothers must also have remembered that day when they sold Joseph as a slave. God has given us a conscience that tells us when we do wrong. If we do not confess our sin and ask God's forgiveness, we will go on feeling guilty for a very long time, as Joseph's brothers did.

READ: GENESIS 41
QUESTIONS:
1. What caused the butler to remember Joseph? (Genesis 41:1, 9)
2. What was the meaning of Pharaoh's dreams? And what advice did Joseph give to Pharaoh? (Genesis 41:28-36)
3. Why did Pharaoh choose Joseph to manage the storage of food? (Genesis 41:38-40)

JOSEPH'S CHOICE TO FORGIVE

Joseph saw his brothers among those who came to buy grain. They did not recognise him. They bowed before him, seeing him as a very important Egyptian ruler. Joseph learned from them that they had a young brother at home with their father. He insisted that when they came again, they must bring Benjamin with them. Making sure that they would return, he kept one of them, Simeon, in prison.

Joseph's brothers did not know that he could understand their language. They spoke to one another about how badly they had treated Joseph, all those years ago. Their consciences troubled them, they felt guilty. Joseph was determined to find out whether his brothers had changed and were sorry for what they had done to him.

The time came when Jacob's family were again short of food. The brothers told their father that they could not go back to Egypt unless Benjamin went with them, to prove that they had spoken the truth to the "important Egyptian". Jacob was very reluctant to let Benjamin go. At last Judah told his father that he would be responsible for Benjamin's safety and so they set off once again.

Joseph had a plan. He would make it appear that Benjamin had stolen something and must stay as a slave in Egypt. Judah spoke to Joseph. He spoke of the grief which his father would suffer if his youngest son did not return. Judah asked to be allowed to take Benjamin's place. He would remain in Egypt and become a slave.

Joseph had his answer. His brothers would not act so cruelly again, as they had done to him. Judah had shown that at last they were truly sorry for what they had done. He sent everyone out of the room, except his brothers and then he made himself known to them. They were very afraid. Joseph was a powerful man now and could have chosen any punishment for them. Instead, he chose to forgive. He explained to them that although they had meant to harm him, God had sent him to Egypt to save them in the time of famine.

Joseph did not have the Bible as we do. But he believed a truth that we can read in the New Testament: "And we know that all things work together for good to those who love God, to those who are called according to His purpose" (Romans 8:28). We know that Joseph understood this, because of his words in Genesis 45:5 and 50:20.

READ: GENESIS 43–44; 50:20
QUESTIONS:
1. What promise did Judah give to his father? (Genesis 43:8-9)
2. Joseph provided a meal for his brothers. What surprised them about the seating arrangement? (Genesis 43:33)
3. What did Judah say that convinced Joseph that his brothers were sorry for their past behaviour and had changed? (Genesis 44:18-33)
4. What did Joseph understand, that helped him to forgive his brothers? (Genesis 50:20)

THE MIDWIVES' BRAVE CHOICE

Shiphrah and Puah were midwives in the land of Egypt, about fifteen hundred years before the birth of the Lord Jesus. They were not Egyptians, but belonged to the people of Israel. Life was hard for all Israelites at that time. The Pharaoh who ruled the country, had forgotten all about Joseph who had saved the Egyptians during seven years of famine.

Pharaoh simply did not like seeing so many Israelites living in his country. He was afraid that they might join the enemies of Egypt and fight against the Egyptians. So he planned to stop their numbers growing. Firstly, he made the Israelites slaves. They had to do really hard work for the Egyptians. Then he ordered the two Hebrew midwives to kill the newborn Israelite boys. Shiphrah and Puah knew that this was wrong. God had spoken long before to Noah, making it clear that it is a sin to take a life (Genesis 9:6).

Pharaoh was powerful. If Shiphrah and Puah disobeyed him, they could be punished or even lose their lives. But the midwives knew that the most important thing was to obey God. They continued to help the mothers and their new babies as they had done before. The lives of the baby boys in their care, were saved.

Pharaoh knew that Shiphrah and Puah had not obeyed him. He sent for them and asked them why they were saving the baby boys. They told Pharaoh that the Israelite babies were born very quickly, before they arrived to help. God knew that these two women had been brave, because they would not do what He had said was wrong. So God looked after Shiphrah and Puah. Pharaoh did not punish them.

The Bible teaches us that we should obey the laws of our country, except when we are told to break God's laws. If that ever happens, we must ask God to help us to do what is right, like Shiphrah and Puah did.

READ: EXODUS 1:1-22
QUESTIONS:
1. What was Pharaoh frightened of? (Exodus 1:9-10)
2. What was the first thing Pharaoh did to make life difficult for the Israelites? (Exodus 1:11-14)
3. What was the second thing Pharaoh did to try to stop the number of Israelites growing? (Exodus 1:15-16)

MOSES CHOSE SUFFERING

Moses belonged to the people of Israel who descended from Abraham. They were named after Abraham's grandson, Jacob, to whom God gave a new name "Israel". Jacob's family moved to Egypt at a time of famine and during that time, their numbers increased greatly. Some years later, there was a new Pharaoh who was afraid that they might one day join with enemies of the Egyptians to fight against them.

Pharaoh enslaved the Israelites and also ordered the killing of their male children. Moses was born during that time, but his life was saved.

He was brought up by Pharaoh's daughter and would have had a privileged life. He knew that his people were the Israelites, who were suffering so much. He thought that they would see him as the leader who could rescue them, but they did not understand this (Acts 7:20-25). We read in the Book of Hebrews that Moses chose to suffer with his people, the Israelites (Hebrews 11:24-26). He refused to go on being treated as the son of Pharaoh's daughter. We can read all about the choice that Moses made, in the Book of Exodus.

Moses left Egypt and lived in the land of Midian for forty years. At the age of eighty, he was told by God that he must go to Pharaoh. He must tell him to allow the Israelites to leave Egypt and hold a feast to God in the wilderness. Pharaoh was not willing to do this and the land of Egypt suffered the terrible plagues that God sent. These plagues were not only a punishment for the Egyptian's cruelty and Pharaoh's refusal to obey God. They showed the uselessness of the idols the Egyptians worshipped.

Eventually, Moses led the Israelites out of Egypt and he remained their leader for forty years. Under God's direction, Moses wrote the first five books of the Bible.

The choice that Moses made, to suffer with his people, led to his amazing life as the leader of God's people. But behind the choice that he made, was God's choice of him, and it was God who gave him strength to lead the Israelites through many years and many difficulties.

READ: EXODUS 1-2; 3:1-10; HEBREWS 11:23-27
QUESTIONS:
1. What was Pharaoh afraid of? (Exodus 1:8-10) and what two things did he decide to do to the Israelites? (Exodus 1:11-14; 15-22)
2. What had God heard and what had God seen? (Exodus 3:7, 9) What did He promise to do? (Exodus 3:8, 10)

PHARAOH: A PROUD CHOICE

The Pharaoh who knew Moses was not the Pharaoh who had been alive in Joseph's time. This new Pharaoh was treating the Israelites very cruelly. He was the one who made them slaves and was responsible for the killing of any boys born to Israelite families.

Moses gave God's message to Pharaoh. He must let the Israelites hold a feast to God in the wilderness. Pharaoh would not want to lose the people who now did a lot of work for the Egyptians. Would he obey God or would he refuse to obey? This was the choice he must make. He was treating the Israelites very cruelly. If he allowed them to travel into the wilderness, would they ever return?

Pharaoh said that he did not know God and he would not let the Israelites go. The results of Pharaoh's choice were terrible for the land of Egypt. The Egyptians were idol-worshippers.

God sent ten plagues upon the land, which showed how useless their idols were. You can read about these plagues in Exodus Chapters 7–12. In the last plague, the oldest son in every Egyptian family died. Before each of the plagues, Moses and his brother, Aaron, visited Pharaoh and told him what would happen if he did not obey God.

Pharaoh hardened his heart and refused to obey, even though God was showing him how powerful He was. Eventually, God gave Pharaoh no more opportunities to change his ways. He must continue in his own wrong choice.

After so many deaths in the tenth plague, Pharaoh sent for Moses in the night. He told him to take all the Israelites and all their possessions out of the land of Egypt. The Egyptians were glad to see the Israelites leave. They had become afraid that they were all going to die.

Even after all that had happened, Pharaoh had second thoughts. He prepared his own chariot and led all the chariots of Egypt in pursuit of the Israelites. When the Israelites saw the Egyptians coming after them, they were afraid. The Red Sea was ahead of them, the Egyptian army was behind them. God made a pathway through the Red Sea and His people were able to cross safely. As Pharaoh and his army followed, the sea came back to its usual course and they were all drowned.

READ: EXODUS 5:1-19; 7:15-25; 12:29-31
QUESTIONS:
1. What was Pharaoh's reply to the message Moses and Aaron brought? (Exodus 5:2)
2. In what way did Pharaoh make the work of the Israelites harder? (Exodus 5: 6-9)
3. What was the last plague and what was the result for the Israelites? (Exodus 12:29-31)

THE PEOPLE'S CHOICE: DISOBEDIENCE

The time had come for the Israelites to make a choice. God had brought them out of slavery in Egypt. He had made a path through the Red Sea for them. They had camped near to Mount Sinai for nearly a year. There God gave them his law – the ten commandments. He also gave them instructions for making the tabernacle – the special tent where God promised to be present with them.

Leaving Sinai, they came near to Canaan – the land God had promised to give them. Would the people obey God and enter the land? God told Moses to send twelve men to spy out the land. They would be able to bring back a report about the land and its people.

The twelve spies spent forty days carefully looking around. They found that crops grew well there, but that the people were very strong and their cities well-fortified. The spies brought their report to Moses and the people. They all agreed that Canaan was a good land. But ten spies made the people afraid by telling them that the Israelites would not be able to overcome the people of Canaan. Only two men, Joshua and Caleb, assured the people that God would help them to take over the land. The people of Canaan were idol-worshippers and very wicked. They had had many years to change their ways but had not done so. God had promised many years before, that He would give their land to the Israelites.

Joshua and Caleb were men of faith. They knew that God was well able to help His people to take possession of the land, no matter how strong the Canaanites were. Would the people listen to them or to the ten spies who were fearful? The people listened to the ten spies and they refused to enter Canaan. The choice that the Israelites made that day, to disobey God, had terrible consequences for them. They had to remain in the wilderness for forty years.

During that time, all those over twenty years old who refused to enter Canaan, would die. They could have had a new life in their own land. Now it would be their children who would one day have what they had lost.

Think about the reason why the Israelites made the wrong choice. Obedience is always linked to faith. Disobedience is always linked to unbelief. God had shown His power in bringing the Israelites out of Egypt and providing for so many people in the wilderness. They should have learned from all that had happened to them, that they had a great God who would not fail them.

The experience of the Israelites is recorded in the Bible so that we will learn from it. Faith in God simply means believing that God will always do what He has promised.

READ: NUMBERS 13:1-3, 17-33; 14:1-10, 30-35
QUESTIONS:
1. How did the ten spies report?
   (Numbers 13:28-29, 31)
2. What did Caleb and Joshua say?
   (Numbers 13:30; 14:6-9)
3. What was the result of disobedience?
   (Numbers 14:30-35)

KORAH CHOSE TO REBEL

Moses did not choose to be the leader of God's people. In fact, when God first spoke to Moses (Exodus 3), Moses thought of several reasons why he could not go to Pharaoh and lead the Israelites out of Egypt. But God had chosen Moses for this task, and God promised to be with him.

After the Israelites left Egypt, they travelled through the wilderness and camped near to Mount Sinai for about a year. There God gave instructions for the making of the tabernacle, the special tent where God met with His people. He also chose Moses' brother Aaron, to be the first High Priest and Aaron's sons to be priests at the tabernacle.

Sometime after leaving Sinai, a man named Korah chose to lead a rebellion against Moses and Aaron. His complaint was that Moses and Aaron had set themselves above the rest of the people, who after all, were all God's people. Moses knew that Korah and those who followed him, were actually rebelling against God. Moses reminded Korah that as a descendant of Jacob's son, Levi, he had been chosen to help in the work of the tabernacle. Surely that was enough for him, without trying to take on a position for which God had not chosen him.

Two other leaders in the rebellion, Dathan and Abiram, accused Moses of acting like a prince over the people. The following day, the people were called together around the entrance to the tabernacle. God told Moses to tell the people to move away from the tents of Korah, Dathan and Abiram. A terrible punishment awaited those three men and the two hundred and fifty others who had followed them. All lost their lives.

We might ask the question, "Why was this rebellion so serious that it had such a dreadful punishment?" To rebel against the man God had chosen, was to rebel against God Himself. We need to remember all that God had done for these people. He had brought them out of a life of slavery in Egypt. He had saved them from Pharaoh's army at the Red Sea. He had provided food and water for them in the wilderness. He had given them His good laws and taught them that while they obeyed Him, He would always be with them and they would know great blessings.

READ: NUMBERS 16:1-35
QUESTIONS:
1. What was the complaint against Moses and Aaron? (Numbers 16:3, 13)
2. What position did Korah already have? (Numbers 16:8-10)
3. What was the punishment of Korah, Dathan and Abiram? (Numbers 16:28-33)

RAHAB: A CHOICE OF FAITH

Rahab lived in Jericho, her house was on the city wall. She lived in days when cities had strong walls, wide enough to build on. The people of Jericho worshipped idols – false gods made out of gold or silver, wood or stone. Rahab was not taught about the true God, the Creator of the universe.

There came a time when Rahab did hear about God. She heard about God drying up the Red Sea when the Israelites came out of Egypt. She heard about victories the Israelites had won. She knew that God was giving the land of Canaan where she lived, to them. She knew that all her people were very afraid of what was going to happen.

Two men came to Rahab's house. They were spies, sent by Joshua to look around the land of Canaan, especially Jericho. (This was forty years after Moses had sent the twelve spies into Canaan.) The king of Jericho heard about this and Rahab was told to hand the men over. Instead of this, Rahab hid the spies on the roof of her house.

Rahab had thought about all she had heard about the Israelite's God. She realised that He was the true God and would certainly help the Israelites to overcome the people of Jericho. Rahab had made her choice. She would help the spies, and then she would ask them to help her. She helped the men to get away safely, but before they left, she asked them to promise that she and her family would be kept safe. They did promise, as long as she did not tell anyone about them and as long as she tied a scarlet cord in her window and kept her family inside her house.

You may already know about the Israelites marching around Jericho and about the walls falling down. (You can read about this in Joshua Chapter 6.) Rahab and her family stayed inside Rahab's house until the two spies came and led them to a place of safety.

The choice that Rahab made, to believe in the true God and to help His people, the Israelites, saved her and her family's lives. It also resulted in Rahab having a place in that wonderful family tree in Matthew 1:5 and 16.

Rahab was not saved because she was a "good" person. She was a sinful woman, but she had faith in God. The Bible teaches us that faith is a gift from God. It was God who helped Rahab to trust in Him, while people around her were still trusting in their useless idols.

READ: JOSHUA 2; JOSHUA 6; MATTHEW 1:5; HEBREWS 11:31
QUESTIONS:
1. What news about the Israelites had Rahab heard? (Joshua 2:10)
2. How do we know that Rahab had come to believe in God? (Joshua 2:11)
3. What were the results of Rahab's choice? (Joshua 6:25; Matthew 1:5; Hebrews 11:31)

ACHAN: A CHOICE OF COVETOUSNESS

The first city in Canaan that the Israelites conquered was Jericho. God had given Joshua the instructions that they must follow. The people obeyed and the walls of Jericho fell. But one man disobeyed one of God's instructions about what to do next.

When the Israelites took over the city, they were not to take anything for themselves. The silver and gold, bronze and iron, were to be dedicated to God. Everything else was to be destroyed.

In Jericho, Achan saw beautiful Babylonian clothing, silver and gold. He wanted them, he took them, and he hid them in the ground under his tent. It seemed that no-one had seen what he had done.

After their victory at Jericho, the Israelites fought against the city of Ai. They were defeated and thirty-six of their soldiers were killed. Joshua was greatly troubled and called upon God. He could not understand why God had not given them another victory. God told Joshua that the defeat was due to sin. Unless that sin was dealt with, God would no longer be with His people to help them.

The following day, Joshua did as God instructed him. The tribes of Israel were brought and God made it clear that the tribe of Judah was guilty. From that tribe, a certain family had to be looked into man by man. At last it was found that the man who had sinned was Achan.

When Joshua asked Achan to confess what he had done, he admitted that he had sinned. He described what was hidden in his tent and the messengers Joshua sent found it just as Achan had said. Achan was put to death.

Achan chose to disobey God. This cost him his life. But that was not all. Achan's sin affected all the people of Israel. The place where Achan was buried was called "The Valley of Achor", which means the valley of trouble.

READ: JOSHUA 6:17-19, JOSHUA 7
QUESTIONS:
1. When Joshua prayed after the defeat at Ai what two things troubled him most? (Joshua 7:8-9)
2. Can you find the four steps Achan took in Joshua 7:21?
3. At Jericho, victory came because of o_ _ _ _ _ _ _ _. At Ai defeat was because of d_ _ _ _ _ _ _ _ _ _ _.

THE GIBEONITES CHOSE TO DECEIVE

Small children often like to dress up, but in the Bible we read about a group of adults who dressed up, to deceive Joshua and the Israelites. These people were from a town called Gibeon. They had heard what had happened to Jericho and Ai, two cities defeated by Israel. So they decided to try to make a peace treaty with the Israelites.

However, the people of Gibeon had a problem. The Israelites had come to take over the land of Canaan, and would not make peace with those who lived there. They needed to convince the Israelites that they came from a far country. So they planned how they could deceive Joshua.

Some men from Gibeon would pretend to be ambassadors from a far country. They must look as if they had been on a long journey, so they put on old clothes and sandals. They took mouldy bread, old sacks and skins of wine. They chose to deceive the men of Israel.

The Gibeonites came to Joshua and the men who were with him. They explained that they had come from a far country to make a peace treaty. The Israelites were not convinced. The Gibeonites showed them their mouldy bread which they said had been fresh when they set off. They pointed out how worn their clothing was.

Joshua made a peace treaty with the Gibeonites, but he had not prayed that God would show him what he ought to do. Three days later the Israelites discovered that the men had come to them from Gibeon in Canaan. Joshua asked them why they had deceived him, and they told him that they were afraid that God would give their land to the Israelites.

Joshua would not break the promise he had made. He would not allow the Israelites to fight against the Gibeonites. The people of Gibeon became servants to the Israelites, but their lives were spared.

READ: JOSHUA 9
QUESTIONS:
1. Why did the Gibeonites "dress up"? (Joshua 9:4-6)
2. What had the Gibeonites been afraid of? (Joshua 9:24)
3. What work would the Gibeonites have to do for Joshua? (Joshua 9:27)

ANOTHER CHOICE FOR THE PEOPLE

Since the death of Moses, Joshua had been a faithful leader. God had chosen him to lead the Israelites into the land of Canaan. Joshua then led the people in the task of conquering the land through many battles. After this, helped by Eleazar the priest and the heads of the twelve tribes, he had divided the land between the tribes.

The time came when Joshua knew that he was nearing the end of his life. He called the people together, so that he could remind them of all that God had done for them. He began by telling them how God had called Abraham to leave a land where false gods were worshipped. He went on to speak of Isaac, and then Jacob who moved with his family to Egypt. Bringing their history up to date, he spoke of the Israelites leaving Egypt and finally entering Canaan. God had been so good to them, they should serve Him and not the false gods of the other nations.

Joshua put a strange choice before the people. He told them that if they would not serve God, they must choose which gods (idols) they would serve. Would it be the idols people worshipped in the land God had called Abraham to leave many years before? Or would it be the idols the people of Canaan had worshipped? Joshua spoke plainly of what he would do: "As for me and my house, we will serve the Lord".

The people understood all that Joshua had told them. The God who had rescued them from slavery in Egypt and had given them the land of Canaan was the only true God whom they must serve. Joshua warned them that if they broke this promise to serve God, then God would punish them.

The people made a solemn promise that they would obey and serve God. Joshua had made them think about the useless idols that other nations served. They did not choose any of those false gods that Joshua had spoken about. The books of the Old Testament following the Book of Joshua, record whether or not the people kept their promise.

READ: JOSHUA 24
QUESTIONS:

1. What did Joshua remind the people of in Joshua 24:2-13?
2. What choice did he say they must make if they would not serve God? (Joshua 24:15)
3. What choice did the people make? (Joshua 24:21-22)

GIDEON AND THE MEN WHO CHOSE TO GO HOME

After Moses and Joshua had died, the people began to forget all that God had done for them. They even bowed down to idols. When this happened, God did not help them against their enemies. When the people were in trouble and called on God, He answered them by raising up leaders called "judges". These leaders led the people to battle against their enemies and also ruled over them when peace was restored.

God chose Gideon to lead the people to victory over the Midianites. The first thing that God told Gideon to do, was to destroy the idols and altars from his father's house. Gideon obeyed. He then called the men from some of the tribes of Israel to come to him. But God told Gideon that there were too many men. The Israelites would think that they defeated their enemies by their strong army. God wanted the people to know that He would save them.

God told Gideon that he must ask anyone who was afraid, to go home. There were 32,000 men in Gideon's army and 22,000 chose to go home. God said that 10,000 was still too many. Gideon must test them by the way they drank water from a stream. Most of the men knelt down to drink, but just 300 scooped up some water in their hands. God said that He would save Israel by the 300 men even though the Midianite army was very large.

Israel had a wonderful victory that day. The 22,000 men who were afraid of the battle, were not there when God chose the 300, so none of them could be chosen. They were not there to see how God dealt with their enemies. What a lot they missed!

If we belong to the Lord Jesus, He wants us to tell others about Him. If we are afraid to do this, we will never learn how God can help us to find the right words, to speak to someone who needs to hear about Jesus.

READ: JUDGES 6:1-14, JUDGES 7
QUESTIONS:
1. What were the Midianites doing that brought great trouble to the people of Israel? (Judges 6:3-5)

2. Why did God tell Gideon that He had too many men with him? (Judges 7:2)
3. What three things did each of the 300 men carry with them? (Judges 7:16)

SAMSON'S CHOICE OF UNHELPFUL PEOPLE

Before Samson was born, his parents knew that God had chosen their son to be a leader in Israel. His mother was told by the angel of the Lord that Samson would begin to free Israel from their enemies, the Philistines. As he grew up, God gave Samson great physical strength.

Even though he knew that God had a special work for him to do, Samson was not careful in choosing people who would be important in his life. He chose to marry a Philistine woman, instead of one from his own nation.

However, this led to Samson beginning to have success against the Philistines, after his father-in-law gave his wife to another man. After his marriage had ended, Samson met another Philistine woman, named Delilah, and he loved her. But Delilah deceived Samson. The Philistines promised her money if she could find out the secret of Samson's great strength. Delilah teased Samson until at last he told her the truth. From the time he was born, Samson's life was controlled by a special promise to God, called a "Nazarite vow". The signs of that promise were that he must not drink any wine or cut his hair.

Samson told Delilah that if his hair was cut, his strength would leave him. Delilah cut Samson's hair while he was sleeping. She then called for the Philistine men. Samson did not know that his strength had gone, and he thought he could escape as he had at other times. His promise was broken and God no longer helped him. Samson became a prisoner of the Philistines, who cruelly blinded him.

The Philistines believed that their false god, Dagon, had brought them victory over Samson. Many of the people were rejoicing in Dagon's temple. Samson prayed for help and God answered his prayer. He gave Samson strength to push against the pillars that supported the temple. The temple fell on the people and many of the enemies of Israel were killed that day.

Hebrews 11:32 lists Samson as a man of faith. He did have faith in God at a time when the Israelites were afraid to fight against their enemies. But his choice of friends did not help Samson to be faithful to God.

READ: NUMBERS 6:1-5; JUDGES 13:1-5; 16:4-31
QUESTIONS:
1. Did the angel promise Samson's mother that her son would conquer the Philistines? (Judges 13:5)
2. Why did Delilah deceive Samson? (Judges 16:5)
3. What did Samson not know? (Judges 16:20)
4. How did Samson's life end? (Judges 16:30)

CHOICES IN THE BOOK OF RUTH
A HUSBAND'S CHOICE AND A WIDOW'S CHOICE

Elimelech and his wife Naomi had their home in Bethlehem, in the southern part of the land of Israel. They had two boys named Mahlon and Chilion. Then came a time of famine, and Elimelech must have thought hard about what he should do to provide for his family at such a time. Should he stay in Bethlehem and face the hardship of shortage of food which could go on for a long time? Or should he take his family away from Bethlehem to a place not affected by the famine?

The Bible does not tell us how Elimelech came to a decision. It does tell us that his choice was to take his family into the land of Moab, on the eastern side of the River Jordan. Sadly, Elimelech was never able to return to the land of Israel because he died in Moab. Naomi was now a widow, but she still had her sons to help her. They both married women who lived in Moab. Mahlon married Ruth and Chilion married

Orpah. Further sorrow came to this family, as Mahlon and Chilion both died. It seemed that Elimelech's choice had brought only trouble to his loved ones. Leaving the land which God had given to the people of Israel was a very serious matter.

Naomi had been in Moab for at least ten years, when news reached her that there was no longer any shortage of food in Israel. She made up her mind that she would go back to Bethlehem. Her two daughters-in-law set out with her. Naomi was concerned about them leaving their country. She told them that it would be better for them to stay in Moab where they might marry again and have their own homes once more. Ruth and Orpah both cried, not wanting to let Naomi go on all alone. Orpah kissed Naomi and returned to her home. Ruth would not leave her mother-in-law and continued with her all the way to Bethlehem.

Naomi's choice, that she would return to the land of Israel, had wonderful results which she could never have dreamed of.

READ: RUTH 1:1-13
QUESTIONS:
1. Why did Elimelech take his family away from their home in Bethlehem? (Ruth 1:1)
2. Why did Naomi decide to return to Bethlehem? (Ruth 1:6)
3. What did Naomi think would be best for her daughters-in-law? (Ruth 1:8-9)

ORPAH AND RUTH

Orpah showed kindness to Naomi, by being willing to go with her to Bethlehem. But for her moving to another country meant leaving family, friends and the idols she had been brought up to worship. Listening to Naomi's advice, she must have thought it was more likely that she would marry again among her own people. She left Naomi and Ruth, and went back to Moab. She had not put her trust in the true God who Naomi worshipped. She went back to the idols worshipped in Moab.

Ruth listened to all that Naomi said about returning to Moab. She told her mother-in-law not to ask her to do such a thing. She was determined to stay with Naomi, live with Naomi's people and trust in Naomi's God. This was Ruth's choice.

Life was not easy for women who had become widows. They had no one to support or protect them. Ruth and Naomi were poor with very little food to eat. God had given a law to the people of Israel, to help the poor people. When it was harvest time, the corners of the fields were to be left with some grain still growing. Also any grain that the reapers dropped was to be left on the ground. Poor people were allowed to follow the reapers and collect whatever they could. This was called "gleaning". This was what Ruth set out to do. It was tiring work under the hot sun.

Ruth gleaned in the field of a man named Boaz. She did not know that this wealthy man was a relation of Elimelech. Boaz was kind to her because he knew how kind she was to Naomi. He also knew that Ruth had come to trust in God. Ruth's choice seemed to have led her into a life of poverty. She did not know that some very wonderful things lay ahead for her.

READ: RUTH 1:14-22; RUTH 2
QUESTIONS:
1. What did Orpah choose to do? (Ruth 1:14-15)
2. Can you find five things that Ruth said she would do? (Ruth 1:16-17)
3. In what ways did Boaz show kindness to Ruth? (Ruth 2:14-16)

2 RELATIONS: 2 CHOICES

Boaz knew that God's law said that when a man died, a near relation could marry his widow and buy his land. There was one man who was a closer relation to Elimelech than Boaz himself. Boaz explained to this relation that he had the right to buy all that had belonged to Elimelech. The man thought that he would do this. But when Boaz explained that he must also take Ruth to be his wife, he said no. His choice was made. He did not want to bring Ruth into his family, even though she was kind, hard-working and truly believed in Israel's God.

Boaz heard about Ruth's kindness to Naomi and also that she now trusted in the true God, not the idols of Moab. When he saw her gleaning in his field, he was kind to her and made sure she had plenty of grain to take home to her mother-in-law. When he knew that Elimelech's nearest relation did not want to act as the kinsman redeemer he was willing to do all that was necessary. ("Kinsman" is another word for a relation. A "redeemer" is someone who pays a price to buy something back.)

When Ruth made her choice to stay with Naomi she did not know that she would become the wife of Boaz. Neither she nor Boaz knew that their names would have a place in a very wonderful family tree. Their son, Obed, became the grandfather of King David, Israel's greatest king. From the family of King David, many years later, the Lord Jesus was born. (See Matthew1:5-6, 16.)

READ: RUTH 3−4
QUESTIONS:
1. What choice did Elimelech's nearest relative make? (Ruth 4:3-6)
2. What choice did Boaz make? (Ruth 4:9-10)
3. What special happiness came to Naomi? (Ruth 4:16)

EXTRA

A "picture" of the Lord Jesus in the Book of Ruth, Boaz was able to act as the "kinsman redeemer" because he was a wealthy man. Boaz was qualified to act as the "kinsman redeemer" because he was a relation. Boaz was willing to be the "kinsman redeemer", to take Ruth into his family.

The Lord Jesus is the Redeemer of everyone who trusts in Him. The price He paid was His own blood shed on Calvary's cross. He is able to be our Redeemer because He is God's own sinless Son. He is qualified to be our Redeemer because He became a man. He is willing to be our Redeemer because of His great love for His people.

HANNAH CHOSE TO PRAY

Hannah was sad. She had a loving husband, Elkanah, but she lived in days when men sometimes had more than one wife. Elkanah had two wives and the name of his other wife was Peninnah. Peninnah was unkind to Hannah, continually reminding her that Hannah had no children, whilst she did. How Hannah longed to have children to love and care for.

Every year, Elkanah took his family to Shiloh, to worship God at the tabernacle. The tabernacle was the special tent that God had given instructions for in the time of Moses. It had been moved from place to place when the Israelites travelled through the wilderness. Once the Israelites settled in the land of Canaan, the tabernacle remained in Shiloh.

During one of their visits to Shiloh, Hannah was so unhappy that she cried and could not eat. When the meal was over, she went on her own to the tabernacle. Still weeping, Hannah prayed. She chose to tell God all about her sorrow. She made a promise that if God would give her a little boy, she would give that boy to God, to serve Him.

Eli, the priest at the tabernacle, was very old. He saw Hannah's lips move, but she prayed silently. Eli did not see her sadness and thought she had drunk too much wine. Hannah explained that she had been telling God all her troubles. Then Eli spoke kindly to her, asking God to answer her prayer.

When Hannah returned to the family, she no longer looked sad. She had prayed and she trusted that God had heard her prayers and would answer her.

God did hear and answer Hannah's prayer. She had a baby boy whom she named Samuel, which means "heard by God" or "asked of God".

We should always follow Hannah's example and choose prayer, instead of worrying about our troubles. And, like Hannah, once we have told God all about what is troubling us, we should trust Him and wait patiently for His answer.

READ: 1 SAMUEL 1:1-28
QUESTIONS:
1. Why was Hannah sad? (1 Samuel 1:6-7)
2. What did Hannah promise? (1 Samuel 1:11)
3. What mistake did Eli make? (1 Samuel 1:13-14)
4. Did Hannah keep her promise? (1 Samuel 1:26-28)

SAMUEL CHOSE TO BE FAITHFUL TO GOD

When Hannah prayed that God would give her a baby boy, she did not know that her son would be chosen by God to lead His people. As soon as he was old enough to leave her, Hannah took Samuel to the tabernacle so that he could learn to help Eli, the priest. While he was still young, God spoke to Samuel, giving him a message for Eli. By the time he had grown up, the people of Israel knew that God had chosen Samuel to be a prophet. A prophet was someone who taught the people the things that God wanted them to know.

The Bible teaches us that God chooses men and women to serve Him. But the Bible also teaches us that we must choose to obey Him. Samuel did this and was faithful to God all through his life.

Samuel was a prophet and he was also the last of the "judges" chosen by God to lead his people. In fact, he led Israel through a time of great change. It was Samuel who received Israel's request for a king. He was not pleased when the people said they wanted a king so that they would be like other nations. Until then, God had chosen men to lead His people, but God Himself was their King. God told Samuel that Israel would have a king. It was Samuel who anointed Saul and introduced him to the people as their first king.

Saul began his reign well, but as time went by, he did not fully obey God. God was displeased with Saul and told Samuel that he had chosen the man who would be king after him. Samuel was sent to Bethlehem, where he anointed David, the youngest son of Jesse.

The Israelites knew that Samuel had done everything he could to help them. He had taught them to keep God's law and that if they did so, God would be with them to provide for them and to help them against their enemies. Even when they had their first king, they asked Samuel to continue to pray for them. He promised that he would do so.

READ: 1 SAMUEL 3:1-10; 8:1-9; 16:1-13
QUESTIONS:
1. Who did Samuel think was calling him? What did Eli tell Samuel to say? (1 Samuel 3:5, 9)
2. What was the people's request? (1 Samuel 8:5)
3. What did God teach Samuel when he went to meet Jesse's sons? (1 Samuel 16:6-7)

DAVID CHOSE TO TRUST GOD

God had chosen David to be Israel's second king, but it would be many years before this came about. He still remained at home, looking after his father's sheep.

King Saul was with his army, facing Israel's enemy, the Philistines. The Philistines had a champion – a man named Goliath who was about three metres tall. He challenged the Israelites to send a man to fight him. They were afraid and no one took up the challenge.

David's three older brothers were among Saul's soldiers. Jesse sent David to find out how his brothers were. He also sent food for the men they were with. David left the sheep with another shepherd, and he set off for the camp as his father had told him. When he arrived at the camp, while he talked with his brothers, he heard Goliath repeating his challenge. David learned that King Saul would reward the man who killed the giant.

David understood that the Israelites were especially God's people and that no one should dare to defy them. David's words were reported to King Saul and he sent for him. David told King Saul that he would go to fight Goliath.

David was young and not trained as a soldier. Saul told him that he could not possibly fight against the Philistine champion. David explained to the king that God had helped him to kill a lion and a bear that attacked his sheep. He was quite sure that God would help him to overcome Goliath.

Saul saw that David was determined, so he put his own armour on him. David was not used to the armour, so he took it off. He chose five smooth stones and with these, his sling and his shepherd's staff, he went towards Goliath. David had made his choice. He would trust the God who had helped him before, to help him now. Goliath was angry. He felt insulted that such a young man should come against him. But one stone from David's sling brought him to the ground. Trusting only in God, David had overcome the man who had caused such fear in the Israelite camp.

READ: 1 SAMUEL 17:1-50
QUESTIONS:
1. When did David learn to trust in God? (1 Samuel 17:34-37)
2. Why did David believe that God would help him to fight Goliath? (1 Samuel 17:26, 36)
3. What did David want other people to know? (1 Samuel 17:45-47)

DAVID CHOSE NOT TO TAKE REVENGE

Saul became jealous of David. He did not like hearing the people praising David because he had killed Goliath. He understood that his own son would never be king if David lived. Saul made more than one attempt to kill David, and also told his son and his servants that they should kill him.

David knew that his life was in danger and that he must go away. He had to move from place to place, because Saul was always trying to find him. A group of men gathered around David and he became their leader. They moved around with him, staying wherever they could.

At one time, David and his men were staying in a cave. Saul entered the cave, but did not see them. Some of David's men tried to persuade him that God was putting Saul into his power, to do whatever he wished.

Stealthily, David approached Saul and cut off a corner of his robe. David told his men that he would not harm the one whom God had chosen to be king. David would not choose revenge, and he would not allow the men who were with him to do Saul any harm.

There was another occasion when David was able to prove to Saul that he would always respect him, as the king whom God had chosen. David knew where Saul and his men had made their camp. At night, David took one man with him and they saw Saul and his soldiers sleeping. David's companion, Abishai, wanted to kill Saul because of the way he had treated David. David would not allow this, but he asked Abishai to take Saul's spear and water jug. They left the camp and David called out from a distance to Saul's general, a man named Abner. He asked Abner why he had not guarded the king properly, seeing he had been able to remove the king's spear.

Saul heard David's voice and made promises never to harm him again. David went on his way. He knew that he could not trust Saul's promise.

READ: 1 SAMUEL 18:6-9; 24:1-22; 26:11, 16
QUESTIONS:
1. What was it that aroused Saul's jealousy against David? (1 Samuel 18:7-9)
2. What was the first proof that David had, that he had spared Saul's life? (1 Samuel 24:4-11)
3. What was the second proof that David had? (1 Samuel 26:11, 16)

JONATHAN CHOSE TO BE A TRUE FRIEND

Jonathan was King Saul's oldest son. He fought very bravely against the Philistines, sometimes with no one with him except his armour-bearer. It is not surprising that after David had killed Goliath, he and Jonathan became firm friends, two courageous young men who both trusted God.

When Jonathan knew that his father was so jealous of David, that he wanted to have him killed, he spoke to his father. He reminded Saul of how David had risked his life when he went against Goliath. David had brought a great victory to Israel. How sinful to kill him when he had done no wrong. Saul promised that David would not be killed.

David knew that Saul's words could not be trusted. Together the two friends made a plan. After Jonathan had again talked with his father, he would give a sign to David as to whether he was in danger or not. They both knew that if Saul was still determined that David should be killed, he would have to go away. At that time the two friends made a covenant (an agreement) that David would always show kindness to Jonathan's family.

The sign was given that David must go away, the two friends must part. The following years were difficult for David. He lived in the wilderness, sometimes in the mountains, sometimes in the forest. A number of men joined him and he was their leader.

Saul was continually searching for David, taking many of his soldiers with him. Once, while David was in the forest, Jonathan came to him. He was able to find his friend, but he did not tell his father. We read that when they met, Jonathan strengthened David's hand in God – he encouraged David to trust in God (1 Samuel 23:16). At this time, Jonathan made it clear that he knew that David would one day be king of Israel. Unlike his father, he felt no jealousy and accepted that David had been chosen by God.

Jonathan chose to be a true, loyal friend to David. This friendship between them is often used as a example of how good, true friendship can be.

READ: 1 SAMUEL 19:1-7; 20:12-42; 23:15-18
QUESTIONS:
1. How did Jonathan try to persuade his father not to harm David? (1 Samuel 19:4-5)
2. What was the sign that Jonathan would give David that meant David would have to go away? (1 Samuel 20:20-22)
3. What did Jonathan encourage David to do and what did he know would happen to David in the future? (1 Samuel 23:16-17)

DAVID'S SERIOUSLY WRONG CHOICE

After pursuing David for many years, King Saul was eventually killed in battle with the Philistines. The people of Judah, the southern part of Israel, then made David their king. Seven years later, David became king over the whole of the nation.

David was a great king. During his reign the enemies of Israel were defeated and the kingdom was made secure. But the Bible is completely truthful. It tells the truth about even the greatest character, including times when they acted wrongly. Even King David chose to act sinfully for a time.

David was a courageous man and was able to lead the people in battle. But there came a day when David sent out his army under their general, Joab, while he remained at home. He saw a very beautiful woman and learned that her name was Bathsheba and that she was married to Uriah, one of David's bravest soldiers. While Uriah was away fighting, David took Bathsheba as his wife. In doing this, he chose to break one of the ten commandments (Exodus 20:14).

Worse followed. David gave instructions to Joab that Uriah should be placed in the most dangerous part of the battle with no one to protect him. Joab sent a message to David telling him that Uriah had been killed. David had not killed Uriah with his own hands, but he had been responsible for his death. Again he was choosing to break God's law (Exodus 20:13).

It seemed that for some time David thought that no one knew what he had done. But God knew and he sent Nathan the prophet to him. When Nathan had spoken to him, David confessed his sin. We know that David was truly sorry for what he had done because of his words in some of the psalms he wrote (Psalm 38 and 51).

David's sinful actions had sad results in his own family, but God forgave his sin. David's words in Psalm 51 have helped many people who have been afraid that God would never forgive their sin.

READ: 2 SAMUEL 12:1-10, 13; PSALM 51
QUESTIONS:
1. How did Nathan set about facing David with his sin? (2 Samuel 12:1-4)
2. How did David respond to Nathan's words? (2 Samuel 12:13)
3. What four things did David ask God to do for him? (Psalm 51:1-2)

ABSALOM: A REBELLIOUS CHOICE

Absalom was one of David's sons and he was a very handsome young man. He lived away from Jerusalem for three years, and when he returned he had a plan to make the people think that he cared about them more than his father did.

Absalom began to drive about in a chariot, with men running ahead to make way for him. Then he would meet anyone who had come to see King David about a difficulty they were in. (At that time, anyone could go directly to the king for his judgement on a disagreement between people.) Absalom told the people that if only he were the judge, he would make sure that they were listened to and have justice. Absalom seemed really interested in the people and they began to think that he would help them more than the king.

Absalom had chosen to lead a rebellion against his father, the king. The first part of his plan was to make himself the people's favourite. When he had done that, he went on to organise the rebellion. Absalom went to Hebron and invited 200 men to join him: they did not know anything of his plans. He also instructed others to be ready to proclaim him king. More people began to join Absalom. A message was sent to David, that many people were following Absalom.

King David left his house in Jerusalem. His servants and many other people who were loyal to him, followed. David had a true friend named Hushai with him. David asked Hushai to return to Jerusalem where he could give advice to Absalom. In fact, he could advise Absalom to act in a way that would really be helping David to put down the rebellion. Hushai did as David had asked him and Absalom thought that his advice was good. Hushai was able to send a message to the king, so that he would know what Absalom was planning to do.

A battle took place between the people loyal to David and those who had joined Absalom. Absalom's men were defeated, but David had given instructions that Absalom should not be harmed. David's general, Joab, and the men with him, killed Absalom in spite of what David had said.

READ: 2 SAMUEL 15:1-15, 33-34; 2 SAMUEL 17:1-16; 2 SAMUEL 18:6-15
QUESTIONS:
1. What was the aim of the first part of Absalom's plan? (2 Samuel 15:2-6)
2. How was Hushai best able to help King David? (2 Samuel 15:33-34 and 17:7, 14)
3. In what way did Joab disobey David? (2 Samuel 18:10-15)
4. How did King David react to Absalom's death? (2 Samuel 18:33)

KING SOLOMON: TWO CHOICES

Before the temple was built at Jerusalem, people went to worship at the tabernacle at Gibeon ten miles north of Jerusalem. Solomon went there early in his reign, and offered many sacrifices on the altar. One night, God appeared to him in a dream. He told Solomon to ask for what he would like God to give him. Solomon asked God to give him wisdom so that he would be able to rule the people well. God was pleased with Solomon's choice, that he had not asked for riches or to be honoured as a great king. God said that he would give Solomon wisdom and that he would also give him what he had not asked for – riches and honour. Then God said that if Solomon obeyed His commandments, He would give him long life as well.

King Solomon's reign started well. God granted his request for wisdom, so that he could rule wisely. In the fourth year of his reign, he began building the temple and it took seven years to complete. When it was completed, a wonderful feast was held and Solomon stood in front of all the people and prayed.

We can read his prayer in 2 Chronicles Chapter 6. He asked that God would always hear His people when they prayed, whatever their trouble or whatever their sin. God answered Solomon. He promised that He would always hear the prayers offered in that temple. God also reminded Solomon that if they disobeyed His laws, He would no longer help them. They would be taken away from their land and the temple would even be destroyed. Above all, the people must not worship the false gods of the nations around them.

Sadly, after the good that Solomon had done, he chose to disobey God. God had told the Israelites that they must not marry women from other nations because this would bring idolatry into Israel. Solomon took many wives from several different nations and as he grew older he began to be involved in the worship of false gods. He provided places for the worship of all the idols his wives bowed down to. God was displeased with what Solomon had done. He said that because Solomon had disobeyed Him, in the days when Solomon's son became king, only the tribe of Judah would be loyal to him.

This happened exactly as God had said. The land was divided into two kingdoms, the southern kingdom of Judah and the northern kingdom of Israel, each one with its own king.

READ: 1 KINGS 3:5-14; 9:1-9; 11:1-13
QUESTIONS:
1. How does 1 Kings 3:9 explain the sort of wisdom Solomon wanted?
2. What had God said that the people of Israel must not do? (1 Kings 9:6-7, 1 Kings 11:1-2)
3. What would be the result of Solomon's disobedience? (1 Kings 11:11-13)

THE QUEEN WHO CHOSE TO SEE FOR HERSELF

King Solomon was the third king of Israel. He was the son of King David. God had given Solomon wisdom to rule the people well. He also gave him great riches.

Solomon's fame spread to other nations, and the Queen of Sheba heard about him. (Sheba was probably in south-west Arabia, present day Yemen.) The queen wondered about the report she heard. Was Solomon really so wise and so great a king?

The Queen of Sheba chose to make the long journey to the land of Israel. This would mean crossing the desert, so she set out with her servants, travelling on camels. Camels were also loaded with costly gifts: gold, spices and precious stones. The queen planned to ask Solomon some very hard questions, to see whether he was really as wise as she had been told.

When she arrived in Jerusalem, the queen soon realised that everything she had heard about King Solomon was true. He really did have great wisdom and he answered all her questions. Everything she saw, Solomon's home, his servants, the food that was prepared, all showed Solomon's power and wealth.

When the Queen of Sheba had been told about King Solomon, she had not believed all that she heard. Now she told him that everything she had seen was even more wonderful than she had been told. She gave Solomon the gifts she had brought with her and he gave gifts to her to take back to her own country.

The Lord Jesus spoke about the visit the Queen of Sheba made to King Solomon. He spoke about the long journey she made to hear Solomon's wisdom. The Lord Jesus is greater and wiser than any king, and yet the Jewish leaders did not understand who He was. He is the Son of God who came from heaven. The Jewish leaders did not give Him the respect that the Queen of Sheba gave to King Solomon.

READ: 2 CHRONICLES 9:1-9, 12; MATTHEW 12:42
QUESTIONS:
1. Why did the Queen of Sheba set out on such a long journey? (2 Chronicles 9:1, 5-6)
2. Who did she say had made Solomon king? (2 Chronicles 9:8)
3. Why did the Lord Jesus say that the Queen of Sheba condemned the Jews who lived in the days when He was on earth? (Matthew 12:42)

REHOBOAM CHOSE TO FOLLOW BAD ADVICE

After the death of Solomon, the people came to Shechem to make Solomon's son, Rehoboam, their king. Jeroboam returned to Israel from Egypt. He had been given a message from God by the prophet Ahijah. The prophet had told him that he would become king over ten of the tribes of Israel. He had gone to Egypt for his own safety, while Solomon remained king. Jeroboam and the people of Israel brought a request to Rehoboam. They said that their lives had been hard during Solomon's reign.

They promised to serve Rehoboam, if he made their lives easier. The king said that he would give his answer after three days.

King Rehoboam spoke to the older men who used to advise his father. He asked them how he should answer the people. They advised him to be kind to the people and then the people would be loyal to him. Rehoboam did not like this advice, so he asked the younger men who had grown up with him, what they thought. The young men said that Rehoboam should make it clear to the people that he would be much harder on them than his father had ever been.

The people came to the king after three days. Rehoboam spoke to them roughly and used the words that his young friends had suggested. The result was that all the people, except the tribe of Judah, which included the small tribe of Benjamin, rebelled against Rehoboam. From that time, the land of Israel was divided between the northern kingdom, known as Israel, and the southern kingdom, known as Judah. This was what God had told Solomon would happen, because of his idolatry.

READ: 2 CHRONICLES 10
QUESTIONS:
1. What was the people's request?
   (2 Chronicles 10:4)
2. What was the advice of the older men?
   (2 Chronicles 10:6-7)
3. What was the advice of the young men?
   (2 Chronicles 10:8-11)

THE KING WHO CHOSE TO SET UP IDOLS

King Saul, King David and King Solomon all reigned over the land of Israel. Things changed during the reign of Solomon's son, Rehoboam. The kingdom was divided, so that Rehoboam reigned in the southern kingdom of Judah, whilst Jeroboam ruled over the northern kingdom of Israel.

Jeroboam was afraid that if the people of Israel went to the temple at Jerusalem, to offer their sacrifices, they would want Rehoboam to be their king again. He thought about how to prevent this and asked advice. He made his choice. He would set up two golden calves as idols for the people to worship. One was placed in Bethel (in the south of his kingdom) and one in Dan (in the north).

When God gave the ten commandments in the time of Moses, the second commandment forbade the worship of idols (Exodus 20:4-5). Idol worship is sinful, and it is also foolish, because idols are completely useless, they cannot see, hear or move. Jeroboam's sinful choice was very serious because it led many people to turn to idolatry, instead of to the God who hears and answers prayer.

God had chosen the family of Moses' brother, Aaron, to be priests and He gave them instructions about their work. Jeroboam chose men to be priests. He also chose a feast day for the people to come and offer sacrifices to the golden calves.

God sent a prophet to Bethel, as Jeroboam was standing by the altar that he had set up for the golden calf. Jeroboam was not pleased to hear the prophet say that his altar would be destroyed. He put out his hand, calling someone to take hold of the prophet.

But God caused Jeroboam's hand to lose its power to move. Jeroboam then asked the prophet to pray for him and when he did so, God healed Jeroboam's hand.

People often aim to be remembered after their death, for something they have done. Jeroboam's sinful choice caused him to be remembered as the king "who made Israel to sin".

READ: EXODUS 20:4-6; 1 KINGS 12:25-33; 13:1-6; PSALM 115:4-8
QUESTIONS:

1. Why did Jeroboam set up idols?
   (1 Kings 12:26-27)
2. What does the second commandment teach?
   (Exodus 20:4-6)
3. What does the Bible say about idols?
   (Psalm 115:4-8)

NAAMAN ALMOST MADE A WRONG CHOICE

Naaman was in charge of the King of Syria's army. He was brave, but had a serious disease called leprosy. Naaman's wife had a young servant girl who had been brought from Israel by Syrian soldiers. She wanted to help Naaman, even though she had been taken captive. The servant girl told Naaman's wife that there was a prophet in Israel who could heal Naaman. Naaman told the king what the girl had said. The king wrote a letter for Naaman to take to the king of Israel.

When the king of Israel read the letter Naaman brought, he was very upset. He knew that he could not heal Naaman. He thought that the king of Syria was planning trouble. Elisha the prophet heard about what had happened. He asked the king to send Naaman to him. Naaman went in his chariot to Elisha's house. He expected Elisha to meet him and call on God to heal him. In fact Elisha just sent a message that Naaman should go and wash seven times in the River Jordan and he would be healed.

Naaman was angry. Elisha had not spoken to him. Why should he wash in the River Jordan when there were two better rivers in Syria? Naaman would have set off for home, but his servants persuaded him to do as the prophet had said. So, Naaman dipped himself in the water seven times. After the seventh time he saw that his illness had gone. He was completely cured.

Naaman's servants had persuaded him to make the right choice. If he had chosen to go home without following Elisha's instructions, he would have remained a leper.

Naaman went back to Elisha's house to give him a present. Elisha would not take anything. It was important for Naaman to understand that it was God who had healed him.

READ: 2 KINGS 5:1-19
QUESTIONS:
1. Why was Naaman angry? (2 Kings 5:9-12)
2. Who helped him to make a wise choice? (2 Kings 5:13)
3. What difference did this healing make to Naaman? (2 Kings 5:15, 17)

GEHAZI CHOSE GREED AND DECEIT

Elisha was chosen by God to be a prophet. One day a man named Naaman came to Elisha. Naaman was in charge of the Syrian army, but he had leprosy. He had been told that the prophet in Israel would be able to heal him.

In 2 Kings Chapter 5 we read about how Naaman was healed. He was so thankful to be free from leprosy, that he wanted to give a present to Elisha. Elisha would not take anything: he knew that it was God who had made Naaman well.

Gehazi, Elisha's servant, decided to get something for himself. He set off after Naaman and when Naaman saw him, he came down from his chariot to meet him. Gehazi said that two young men had come to Elisha, and Elisha had sent him to ask for some silver and some clothing for each of them. None of this was true. Gehazi had chosen to tell lies as a way of getting what he wanted. Naaman willingly gave Gehazi more than he had asked for, and sent servants to carry the gifts for him. But Elisha knew what had been done. Gehazi said that he had not been anywhere, but Elisha knew that was a lie. Naaman had been healed of leprosy, but Gehazi became a leper.

Leprosy was a serious illness in those days and there was no medicine to cure it. Gehazi's lies and greed had a very serious punishment, because his sin was very serious. He had broken the last of the ten commandments by being greedy, or covetous. He had told lies to Naaman and to Elisha, breaking another commandment. Worst of all, he had brought the name of God's prophet into what he had done, saying that Elisha had sent him.

Elisha had been careful to make Naaman understand that the power to heal was not his, but God's. It was also important that Naaman saw his healing as God's gift, not something he could pay for. This true story of Naaman, reminds us that we can do nothing to deserve God's forgiveness or to earn eternal life with Him (see Romans 6:23).

READ: 2 KINGS 5:16, 20-27; EZEKIEL 18:30; 1 JOHN 1:9
QUESTIONS:
1. Find the things that Gehazi did or planned to do, that were wrong in 2 Kings 5:20, 22, 25.
2. Why would Elisha not accept anything from Naaman? (2 Kings 5:16)
3. What should Gehazi have done when Elisha spoke to him about his sin? (1 John 1:9 and Ezekiel 18:30) c _ _ _ _ _ _ and r _ _ _ _ _ .

ENDORSEMENTS

Our choices matter. The "big" choices grown-ups make are practiced in the thousands of little choices we make as we grow. The Old Testament is a collection of stories that can guide our choices (1 Corinthians 10:11). It is also part of a single story that tells how God was working out his free and gracious choice to make a kingdom of loyal friends from a world of lost sinners. This book can help children choose well and, most importantly, trust in the God who redeems our choices—even the bad ones—as He unfolds His beautiful plan.

WILLIAM BOEKESTEIN, AUTHOR OF *SHEPHERD WARRIOR*, A STORY FOR YOUNG READERS ABOUT ULRICH ZWINGLI

Jean Stapleton has compiled a clear and thought-provoking devotional for children contrasting biblical characters who chose things such as forgiveness, obedience, or suffering with characters who sadly chose things such as deception, greed, or compromise. This book is an excellent aid for helping children evaluate situations they may face and understand the agency they possess as a child of God to choose what will be God-honoring.

HEATHER LEFEBVRE, AUTHOR OF *THE HISTORY OF CHRISTMAS*

MORE BOOKS BY JEAN STAPLETON

More Good Choices, Bad Choices

40 Bible Characters Decide

Jean Stapleton

More Good Choices, Bad Choices
40 Bible Characters Decide
Jean Stapleton

The Bible teaches us that God always does what He says He will do. It is a great comfort to know, that God's plans and purposes are not changed by men and women who make wrong or foolish choices. In a way that we cannot understand, God rules over everything, so that His promises are always fulfilled. Young and old, rich and poor all appear in the Bible and through them we see examples of people who made wise and foolish decisions. This book will help you to focus on God's Word and his wisdom guiding you in your own day to day choices.

ISBN: 978-1-5271-0528-7

GIRLS JUST LIKE YOU

Bible Women who Trusted God

JEAN STAPLETON

Girls Just Like You
by Jean Stapleton

We might think that people in Bible times were different from us (much braver and better than we are), but that isn't true. They were just like us – just like you, in fact!

There are fifty different stories in this book, with Bible verses to read that will teach you about the girls and women in the Bible who trusted God. Find out about them and about yourself by discovering God's Word that He has written for you!

ISBN: 978-1-78191-997-2

BOYS JUST LIKE ME
Bible Men who Trusted God

JEAN STAPLETON

Boys Just Like Me
by Jean Stapleton

We might think that people in Bible times were different from us (much braver and better than we are), but that isn't true. They were just like us – just like you, in fact!

There are fifty different stories in this book, with Bible verses to read that will teach you about the boys and men in the Bible who trusted God. Find out about them and about yourself by discovering God's Word that He has written for you!

ISBN: 978-1-78191-998-9

CHRISTIAN FOCUS PUBLICATIONS

Christian Focus | Christian Heritage | CF4K | Mentor

Christian Focus Publications publishes books for adults and children under its four main imprints: Christian Focus, CF4K, Mentor and Christian Heritage. Our books reflect our conviction that God's Word is reliable and Jesus is the way to know him, and live for ever with him.

Our children's publication list includes a Sunday School curriculum that covers pre-school to early teens, and puzzle and activity books. We also publish personal and family devotional titles, biographies and inspirational stories that children will love.

If you are looking for quality Bible teaching for children then we have an excellent range of Bible stories and age-specific theological books.

From pre-school board books to teenage apologetics, we have it covered!

Find us at our web page:
www.christianfocus.com

CF4•K
Because you're never
too young to know Jesus